DIGITAL CITIZENS

MY DIGITAL WORLD

BEN HUBBARD

ILLUSTRATED BY DIEGO VAISBERG

Lerner Publications ◆ Minneapolis

First American edition published in 2019 by Lerner
Publishing Group, Inc.

First published in Great Britain in 2018 by
The Watts Publishing Group
Copyright © The Watts Publishing
Group 2018

Credits
Series Editor: Julia Bird
Illustrator: Diego Vaisberg
Packaged by: Collaborate

Lerner Publications Company
A division of Lerner Publishing Group, Inc.
241 First Avenue North
Minneapolis, MN 55401 USA

For reading levels and more information, look up
this title at www.lernerbooks.com.

Main body text set in Courier PS Std.
Typeface provided by Monotype Typography.

Library of Congress Cataloging-in-Publication Data

The Cataloging-in-Publication Data for *My Digital World*
is on file at the Library of Congress.
ISBN 978-1-5415-3883-2 (lib. bdg.)
ISBN 978-1-5415-4310-2 (eb pdf)

Manufactured in the United States of America
1-45066-35893-7/17/2018

CONTENTS

What Is Digital Citizenship?   4

Connect, Collect, and Communicate   6

A World of Websites   8

Cyber Searching   10

Digital Friendships   12

To Share or Not to Share?   14

Messaging Aware   16

Phone Etiquette   18

Cyberbullying   20

Bystanding   22

Send a Cyber Smile   24

A World Outside   26

Digital Quiz   28

Glossary   30

Helpful Websites   31

Index   32

WHAT IS DIGITAL CITIZENSHIP?

When we log onto the internet, we become part of a giant online world.

In this world we can use our smartphones, tablets, and computers to explore, create, and communicate with billions of different people. Together, these people make up a global digital community. That is why they are known as digital citizens. When you use the internet you are a digital citizen too. So what does this mean?

CITIZEN VS DIGITAL CITIZEN

A good citizen is someone who behaves well, looks after themselves and others, and tries to make their community a better place. A good digital citizen acts exactly the same way. However, the online world is bigger than just a local neighborhood, city, or country. It spans the whole world and crosses every kind of border. It is therefore up to all digital citizens everywhere to make this digital community a safe, fun, and exciting place for everyone.

MY DIGITAL WORLD

Often we talk about the online world as though it is different from the real world. However, the two are closely linked. In reality we merge the two worlds by using aspects of the internet in our everyday lives. This book explores how we use the internet, why we use it, and what we do while we're there. Together all of these elements make up your digital world.

CONNECT, COLLECT, AND COMMUNICATE

Can you imagine life without the internet?

The internet is how we communicate using messages written out in text. It is how we collect information from websites. It is where we go to listen to music, watch films, and play games. We even do our shopping there. For digital citizens, the internet is part of everyday life.

SEE YOU AT THE BUS STOP IN 10 MINUTES.

CONNECT

All we need to go online is a digital device and an internet connection. Handheld devices such as smartphones and tablets have made this easy. We connect these devices to the internet using a signal from our mobile phone provider or by using Wi-Fi, a wireless internet connection. This means many people are constantly connected to the internet wherever they go.

COLLECT INFORMATION

The internet has made finding information easier than at any time in history. In a few clicks we can find a bus schedule, look at a weather forecast, and see what's on TV. It's also very helpful for homework!

COMMUNICATE

Having a handheld digital device that is constantly connected has changed the way we communicate. Now we can have almost instant access to friends and family by making a video call or sending them an email, social media message, or instant message. Sometimes it seems many of us spend more time messaging each other than talking.

SEND ME A TEXT IF YOU'LL BE LATE HOME FROM SCHOOL.

CAN YOU FORWARD THAT EMAIL FROM DAISY TO ME?

GRAN SAYS SHE'LL SKYPE TONIGHT AT 7.

A WORLD OF WEBSITES

Websites are where we go to discover new things, read about our favorite subjects and fill our heads with facts.

For example, did you know there are over one billion websites in the online world? With so many options, how do we know which are safe for kids to visit?

WHAT IS A WEBSITE?

Each website is made up of a collection of web pages. Every time we click on a web page, packets of information from the website are sent to our computer. But often we don't know who is controlling the website. This means we have to be careful about trusting what we read.

CHOOSE BEFORE YOU CLICK

Clever digital citizens get their information from trustworthy websites. The suffix, or three letters at the end of a website, is the first clue to what it is about. These show you if the website is there to provide information, make money, or has an unspecified purpose. The most common suffixes are:

1 .edu—an educational institution, such as a school or university

WHICH WEBSITE IS ALRIGHT?

Not all websites are right for kids. Some have inappropriate, violent, or upsetting content. Others are fake sites that are designed to scam or steal from people. Clever digital citizens choose which websites they visit.

The simplest way to find kid-friendly sites is to get a list from your school. The other way—you guessed it—is to go online. The following sites contain lists of dozens of websites for kids only. Check them out:
https://www.commonsensemedia.org/lists/kid-safe-browsers-and-search-sites
https://www.todaysparent.com/family/30-fun-and-safe-kids-websites/
http://www.kidsites.com

IF YOU GET YOUR INFORMATION FROM SOCIAL MEDIA SITES AND BLOGS IT'S OFTEN INCORRECT. TRY THIS ENCYCLOPEDIA WEBSITE. IT SAYS THE POP STAR IS 21.

2 .gov—a government website

3 .org—usually a non-profit site, such as a charity

4 .com—a commercial site that is designed to make money

5 .net—a website without a specified purpose

CYBER SEARCHING

Only 30 years ago people found most of their information using books, magazines, and newspapers.

Doing homework often meant a visit to the local library. Today, information about almost anything is only a few clicks away. However, we have to be careful about where we look.

SAFE SEARCHING

Searching the internet is fantastic fun, but it's good to have a trusted adult around when you do it. They can help you decide what keywords to type into your search engine and set up filters that block out any bad websites. There are also search engines just for kids such as:
http://www.safesearchkids.com
http://www.kiddle.co
http://www.kidzsearch.com
http://www.swiggle.org.uk

As well as kid-friendly search engines, there are also child versions of some adult websites. Some of these are:
http://kids.britannica.com/
https://kids.youtube.com
http://www.natgeokids.com/

YOU CAN FIND ALMOST ANYTHING ON THE INTERNET TODAY.

ELEPHANTS FLYING AIRPLANES: 5,580,000 WEB PAGES.

SMALLEST SAXOPHONE IN THE WORLD: 1,170,000 WEB PAGES.

KEY WORDS

Using a few keywords will get you to the best information fast. You don't need to type full sentences. Try typing the highlighted keywords from this sentence into a kid-friendly search engine to try: What is the longest river in Africa?

WEBSITE CHECK

Did you know you can check out a website before you even click on it? You can do this by putting the website's name into a search engine and adding "reviews." This can show if anyone has had trouble with it in the past. Remember that if you end up on a website that you don't like for any reason, you can just click out.

WHY ARE SOME OF THESE WEBSITES BLOCKED?

BECAUSE THEY HAVE NASTY STUFF THAT MIGHT UPSET YOU.

FAIR ENOUGH, I'VE ALREADY SEEN SOME STUFF I DON'T LIKE!

DIGITAL FRIENDSHIPS

Social media is often how we keep in touch with friends and family.

Social media sites are like online clubs where we can post information, photos, and blogs for other people to comment on. It can be a great way to connect with people, but we must be careful to protect ourselves at the same time.

PERSONAL AND PRIVATE

Keeping our personal information secret is important when we're online. This includes details such as your real name, address, and phone numbers. We protect this information by using passwords on our email and social media accounts. We must keep our passwords secret, even from our best friend. We also have to be careful to protect our friends' personal information.

YOU'LL NEED TO PICK A NAME AND PICTURE. HOW ABOUT ONE OF YOUR FAVORITE VIKING CHARACTERS?

GOOD IDEA!

PASSWORD PROTECT

Strong passwords contain a mixture of numbers, symbols, and uppercase and lowercase letters that only you know. Twelve-year-old Dan who likes cats could choose something like:

1   *SWALC
(asterisk symbol +
CLAWS spelt backward)

ONLINE IDENTITY

To avoid using our real identity on the internet, we can instead create an online profile. On social media sites this means choosing a screen name and an avatar, or screen face. Creating an online profile can be great fun. You can pick any name you want and a picture of anything you like to represent you.

HELLO, I'M 09THOR, BLOODTHIRSTY WARRIOR.

2 Danoiboy12
(the nickname only his sister uses + his age)

3 !!!
(three exclamation marks for the number of goals he scored last year)

4 = *SWALCDanoiboy!!!

TO SHARE OR NOT TO SHARE?

For most of the last century, people had to write a letter to tell others what they'd been up to. Now we can post every aspect of our daily lives instantly to our social media accounts. However, what is appropriate information to share, and how do we know if we are sharing too much?

THIS IS THE SHOP WHERE I'M GOING TO BUY LUNCH.

THESE ARE THE SANDWICH OPTIONS.

TOO MUCH INFORMATION

We all know people who seem glued to their social media accounts. Every day there are dozens of posts and photos about what they are doing and how they are feeling. Sometimes it can become a bit too much. Every digital citizen has the right to post whatever they want online. But sometimes it's also good to pause before you post and ask yourself the question: "Is this really worth sharing with others?"

SO? WHAT HAPPENED?

HE CHOSE HAM AND CHEESE.

SHARING SAFELY

To share safely with people on social media, the first priority is to protect our personal information. This includes details about our future plans that could be used against us. For example, writing a post about an upcoming holiday that includes the dates you will be away is like telling the world that your house will be empty during that time. It's also important not to post details of where you are going to be on a particular day. You don't know who the information could be forwarded to.

MESSAGING AWARE

Emails and instant messaging are the main method of communication for many of us.
Even if your phone and tablet are on silent mode, you can still message your friends. And once you've read the message you can delete it forever, right? Wrong. Everything we do online lives on in cyberspace.

ME
MR. HUMPHREYS IS SOOO BORING. AND HE SMELLS.

SUE
AND DID YOU SEE HIS AWFUL TIE TODAY?

ME
I DIDN'T DO ANY HOMEWORK LAST NIGHT. CAN'T BE BOTHERED.

SUE
I HOPE YOUR DAD DOESN'T FIND OUT.

ME
HE LETS ME DO WHAT I WANT. LEAST I'M NOT A TEACHER'S PET LIKE JESS.

SUE
I KNOW. MUST BE BORING TO BE SOOO BRAINY.

DIGITAL FOOTPRINT

Everything you do online leaves a trail called a digital footprint. Your digital footprint is a record of your internet activity. It shows what you searched for, which websites you visited, what you wrote in messages, and what you posted. Your digital footprint can only be seen by computer experts, but it is a permanent record—once it is recorded, it is almost impossible to delete.

Messages on phone screen:

ME
'MR HUMPHREYS IS SOOO BORING. AND HE SMELLS.'

SUE
'AND DID YOU SEE HIS AWFUL TIE TODAY?'

ME
'I DIDN'T DO ANY HOMEWORK LAST NIGHT. CAN'T BE BOTHERED.'

SUE
'MIND YOUR DAD DOESN'T FIND OUT.'

ME
'HE LETS ME DO WHAT I WANT. LEAST I'M NOT A SWOT LIKE JESS.'

SUE
'I KNOW. MUST BE BORING TO BE SOOO BRAINY.'

WHAT WOULD MOM SAY?

Once we send on a message, it goes out into cyberspace and we lose control of it. It could be forwarded to someone else, seen by other people on a friend's phone, or stolen if your account is hacked. The simplest thing is to make sure your messages are polite, kind, and wouldn't offend anyone. A good rule of thumb for writing a message is: could you show it to your mom? If not, don't send it.

PHONE ETIQUETTE

In the modern world, many of us are constantly glued to our smartphones and tablets.

Instead of talking to each other, we often send a message instead. Clever digital citizens use their digital devices as communication tools—not to replace real interactions. Here are some guidelines for good "phone etiquette."

RESPECT THE LIVING

When you are with someone else, keep your texting, messaging, and phone calls to a minimum. Otherwise it's like telling your companion they are less important than everyone else.

SWOOOOSHHH

YOU GOING TO LETI'S B'DAY?

MAYBE. I HAVE TO ASK MY MOM.

TRY TALKING, NOT TEXTING

Messaging is a great way to keep in touch, but long messaging conversations can be time consuming and unnecessary. Sometimes a short phone call is the simplest option. It also means you are interacting with a live person!

ALL RIGHT?

LOT'S GOING ON. WHERE DO I START? COULDN'T FIND MY SHOES TODAY AND THEN I FORGET MY LUNCH, MY SISTER HOGGED THE BATHROOM ...

SWITCH IT OFF

There are some places where even a phone on silent mode can be irritating for others around us. These include places like cinemas or at a family dinner. Using your phone in the classroom is almost always a bad idea. Good digital citizens learn when to switch their phones off and be considerate of other people.

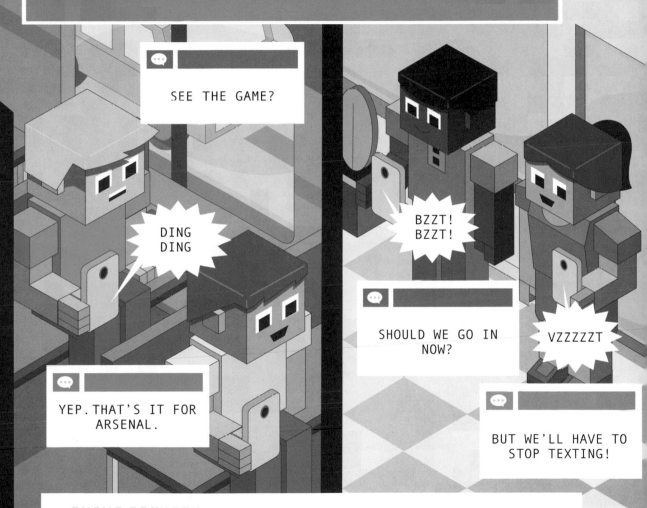

SEE THE GAME?

DING DING

BZZT! BZZT!

YEP. THAT'S IT FOR ARSENAL.

SHOULD WE GO IN NOW?

VZZZZZT

BUT WE'LL HAVE TO STOP TEXTING!

PHONE PRIVACY

Talking loudly on your phone, having alerts that go off all the time, or playing music in public is not good phone etiquette. In these situations, it is best to keep conversations short and plug in your headphones.

CYBERBULLYING

Have you ever been the victim of cyberbullying?

Cyberbullies are people who pick on others online. They use email, instant messaging, and social media to write hurtful and aggressive messages. Cyberbullying can happen to anyone at any time.

The problem with cyberbullying is that it is hard to ignore. Once online we can be attacked anywhere at any time of day or night—even in our own bedrooms! This can make us feel isolated, alone, and unable to escape.

NO ONE
LIKES YOU!

YOU ARE GOING
TO GET IT AT
SCHOOL TOMORROW!

EVERYONE'S LAUGHING
AT YOU.

STOP THE CYBERBULLY!

You can feel helpless if you are being cyberbullied. Following these steps can help you take back control.

1 Report the cyberbullying to your trusted adult. They may contact your school and even the police.

2 Take screen shots of the cyberbully's messages as evidence.

The thing to remember about cyberbullying is that you are not alone. Millions of people have been the victim of cyberbullying. It is important that you don't keep it a secret. Instead, tell your family and friends what has happened. This is the first step to stopping the cyberbullying and making yourself feel better.

THE SAME THING HAPPENED TO MIA A FEW DAYS AGO.

LOOK, THIS CAME IN LAST NIGHT.

THAT'S HORRIBLE! WHO WOULD DO THAT?

I'M REALLY SORRY TO HEAR ABOUT THE CYBERBULLYING. LET'S HAVE A CHAT AND SORT THIS OUT.

3 Don't reply to the cyberbully's messages, even if it is tempting to do so.

4 Block the cyberbully on your social media accounts and press the "report abuse" button if there is one.

5 Tell your friends what is going on. It is better to share than keep cyberbullying a secret.

BYSTANDING

Part of being a good digital citizen is protecting other people from being bullied online.

Some people say "it's not my problem" and watch this type of harassment continue. Others step in to support the person being bullied.

BYSTANDERS

A bystander is someone who watches something bad happening but does nothing to help. When cyberbullying takes place, a bystander says it is none of their business or that they can't be bothered to get involved.

YOUR TRAINERS ARE UGLY.

GET A HAIRCUT!

BILLY NO-FRIENDS IS HERE.

THIS IS HORRIBLE. THEY'RE GANGING UP ON SAM AGAIN.

UPSTANDERS

Upstanders are people who step in to show their support for a victim of cyberbullying. They report the abuse to a trusted adult, their school, the social media site where it is happening, and sometimes the police. Just letting the bullied person know you are on their side can also make a huge difference.

PEER PRESSURE

Sometimes cyberbullies encourage others to join in and pick on someone together. This often means forwarding or "liking" nasty online messages about the victim, or passing on their online details so others can bully them too. This is peer pressure and it can make life unbearable for the person being picked on. When this happens, the role of an upstander is more important than ever.

I'VE JUST SEEN SOME OF THE MESSAGES BEING POSTED. ARE YOU OK?

WHOEVER SENDS THESE IS A COWARD.

SEND A CYBER SMILE

As a member of the new generation of digital citizens, you will help decide what the online world will be like in the future.

How you behave online will have an impact on this. Digital citizens can make the online world a happy and encouraging place simply by being friendly and sending people a cyber smile.

> DID YOU KNOW THAT AGGIE'S SICK WITH A NASTY BUG THIS WEEK? WE SHOULD TEXT HER A NICE MESSAGE.

> THAT'S A GREAT IDEA!

CYBER SMILES

When you communicate with others online, it's easy to forget there is another real person involved. But at the end of another digital device is a human being just like you, with feelings and hopes and needs. Sometimes finding a nice thing to say to them can make all the difference to their day.

NEVER GET PERSONAL

Even if you strongly disagree with something someone has said online, it's best to never make it personal. This means telling them you disagree with what they said, not saying that they are stupid or ignorant. Otherwise it can quickly turn into "flaming," which means trading insults. This never gets anyone anywhere.

THANKS FOR BEING SUCH A GREAT FRIEND, AGGIE. I HOPE YOU'RE WELL BY THE WEEKEND SO WE CAN HANG OUT!

GET BETTER, AGGIE, WE MISS YOU OUT HERE!

MISTAKES ARE HUMAN!

We have all said things in the heat of the moment that we regret after calming down. If you have done this online, you can make amends. The best way to do this is to apologize to the person you have offended and take down the message, post, or blog that has done that immediately.

A WORLD OUTSIDE

Being a digital citizen is great fun and it's important too.

The internet is here to stay and will make up a big part of your future. However, having time off being online is also important. Sometimes, when we take a break from the internet, we rediscover all the other things there are to enjoy.

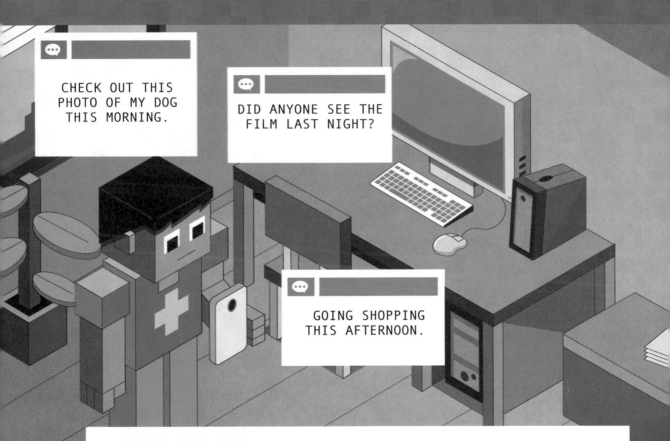

CHECK OUT THIS PHOTO OF MY DOG THIS MORNING.

DID ANYONE SEE THE FILM LAST NIGHT?

GOING SHOPPING THIS AFTERNOON.

GOING OFFLINE

It can make us feel weird, disconnected, and even vulnerable, but taking an internet break and going offline is a smart move sometimes. Experiment by switching off all your digital devices and leaving the house without your phone. You could also try having a phone-free day outside with your friends. It can be a very freeing experience.

DO I NEED TO LOOK?

Often we pick up our phones because we are bored or don't know what to do next. But we should ask ourselves: was there really a good reason to be using it? It's OK to leave your phone in your pocket or even switch it off for a while.

HOW ABOUT TURNING OUR PHONES OFF FOR A BIT?

GREAT IDEA!

BUT I'LL MISS OUT!

Because we are so used to being connected all the time, it can feel like you'll miss something important if you go offline for a while. However, when we go back online we find the world is much the same as when we left it. If you are really worried, leave a message on your email account or social media wall that you're taking a break from the internet.

DIGITAL QUIZ

Now that you've reached the end of this book, how do you feel about your digital world?

How much have you learned? And how much can you remember? Take this quiz and tally up your score to find out.

1. What should you do if you see someone being cyberbullied?

a. Switch off your phone and take out the battery

b. Make friends with the bully

c. Tell a trusted adult

2. What will happen if you switch off your phone for the day?

a. All of your "friends" will delete you

b. The world will come to an end without warning

c. You'll have some uninterrupted time to do something else

3. Which of these is interesting information to share on social media?

a. What you had for breakfast

b. How you felt at 11:17 this morning

c. A photo from your skydiving adventure

4. Which keywords will best get you information about "what fish eat?

a. Fish/seaweed/food

b. Fish/food/eat

c. Food/fish/chips

5. What is the name of the trail we leave behind when we go online?

a. Digital footprint

b. Digital handstand

c. Digital footstep

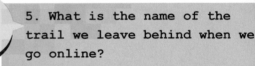

6. Which of these would you send to give someone a cyber smile?

a. A compliment

b. A suggestion that they go to the dentist

c. A blank email

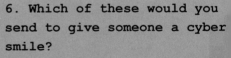

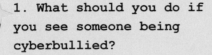

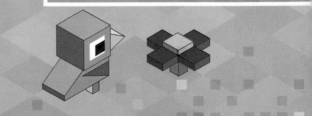

7. How often should you use your phone when hanging out with a friend?

a. As often as possible
b. Every 15 minutes only
c. As little as possible— you have a live friend to be with

8. Which of these is a good reason to look at your phone?

a. It's been three minutes since you last looked at it
b. You're bored and don't know what to do
c. Someone is calling you

HOW DID YOU DO? ADD UP YOUR SCORE TO SEE.

1-4: You are on your way, but retake the quiz to get a score over 4.

5-7: You've passed the quiz well. Now see if you can pass the quiz in the book *My Digital Community and Media*.

8: Wow! 8 out of 8. You are a natural born digital citizen!

ANSWERS

1: c; 2: c; 3: c; 4: b; 5: b; 6: a; 7: a; 8: c

GLOSSARY

avatar
A computer icon or image that people use to represent themselves online

block
A way of stopping someone from sending you nasty messages, emails, or texts online

cyberbullying
Bullying that takes place online or using internet-based apps

digital
Technology that involves computers

etiquette
The rules for behaving politely in society

hacker
A computer experts who breaks into computers and computer networks online

instant messaging
Apps that allow for text messages to be sent via the internet

internet
The vast electronic network that allows billions of computers from around the world to connect to each other

online
Being connected to the internet via a computer or digital device

screen name
Also known as a username, a screen name is a made-up name used to disguise your real identity, which is used for your online accounts

search engine
A computer program that carries out a search of available information on the internet based on the words you type in

smartphone
A mobile phone that is capable of connecting to the internet

social media
Websites that allow users to share content and information online

trusted adult
An adult you know well and trust who can help you with all issues relating to the internet

website
A collection of web pages that is stored on a computer and made available to people over the internet

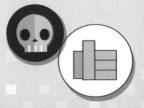

HELPFUL WEBSITES

Digital Citizenship
The following websites have helpful information about digital citizenship for young people:

http://www.digizen.org/kids/

http://www.digitalcitizenship
.nsw.edu.au/Prim_Splash/

http://www.cyberwise.org
/digital-citizenship-games

Bullying
These websites have excellent advice for kids who are experiencing bullying online:

https://www.childline.org.uk
/info-advice/bullying-abuse
-safety/types-bullying/online
-bullying/

http://www.bullying.co.uk

https://www.stopbullying.gov
/kids/facts/

Staying Safe
These websites are dedicated to keeping kids safe online, with lots of good advice:

http://www.childnet.com/young
-people/primary

http://www.kidsmart.org.uk

http://www.safetynetkids.org
.uk/personal-safety/staying
-safe-online/

http://www.bbc.co.uk
/newsround/13910067

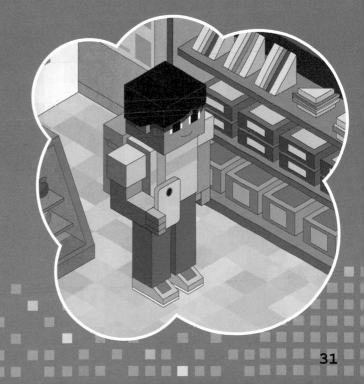

INDEX

abuse, reporting,
    20–21, 23
apologizing, 25
avatars, 13

bullying, 20–23
bystanding, 22–23

cyberbullying,
    20–23

digital
    footprint,
    16–17

etiquette, 18–19

information,
    protecting
    personal,
    12–13, 15

kindness,
    showing, 24–25

messaging,
    instant, 7,
    16–18, 20

offline, time,
    26–27
over posting,
    14–15

passwords,
    creating, 12–
    13
peer pressure, 23
privacy,
    protecting,
    12–15
profiles, online,
    13

search engines,
    using, 10–11
sharing
    information,
    14–15
suffixes, 8–9
switching off,
    19, 26–27

upstanders, 23

websites,
    trustworthy,
    6, 8–9